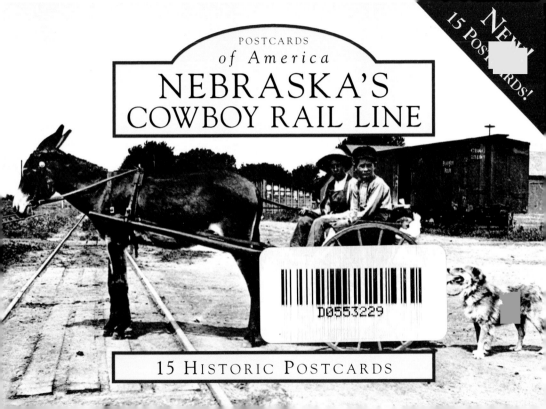

POSTCARDS
of America

NEBRASKA'S
COWBOY RAIL LINE

NEW
15 POSTCARDS!

D0553229

15 HISTORIC POSTCARDS

Published by Arcadia Publishing
Charleston SC, Chicago IL, Portsmouth NH, San Francisco CA

For all general information contact Arcadia Publishing at:
Telephone 843-853-2070
Fax 843-853-0044
E-mail sales@arcadiapublishing.com
For customer service and orders:
Toll-Free 1-888-313-2665

Visit us on the Internet at www.arcadiapublishing.com

The Fremont, Elkhorn and Missouri Valley Railroad came into being on January 20, 1869. Construction on the line, which would eventually reach more than 400 miles across the state, started the same year. (Courtesy of the Dodge County Historical Society.)

Excerpted from Images of Rail: Nebraska's Cowboy Rail Line, published by Arcadia Publishing © 2009 Keith Terry.

PUBLISHED BY ARCADIA
WWW.ARCADIAPUBLISHING.COM

STANTON   NEBRASKA'S COWBOY RAIL LINE

Two attempts were made to run a line into Stanton before the Fremont, Elkhorn and Missouri Valley Railroad got there. This photograph was taken about 1912. (Courtesy of the Historical Society of Stanton County.)

Excerpted from Images of Rail: Nebraska's Cowboy Rail Line, published by Arcadia Publishing. © 2009 Keith Terry.

PLACE
STAMP
HERE

PUBLISHED BY ARCADIA
WWW.ARCADIAPUBLISHING.COM

In 1872, John Neligh, a West Point merchant who had earlier helped to attract rail service to that town, purchased property along the Elkhorn River in Antelope County. The train arrived in the town named after John Neligh in October 1880. (Courtesy of Bardeene Glandt.)

Excerpted from *Images of Rail: Nebraska's Cowboy Rail Line*, published by Arcadia Publishing © 2009 Keith Terry.

PUBLISHED BY ARCADIA
WWW.ARCADIAPUBLISHING.COM

In early July 1885, the iron highway reached the community of Hay Springs, which probably resulted in some memorable Independence Day celebrations. The community apparently drew its name from the abundant hay that grew in the area and a spring that provided life-giving water to locals. (Courtesy of George Christensen.)

Excerpted from Images of Rail: Nebraska's Cowboy Rail Line, published by Arcadia Publishing © 2009 Keith Terry.

PUBLISHED BY ARCADIA
WWW.ARCADIAPUBLISHING.COM

GLEN.

In some places, depots were little more than converted boxcars and that was the case in Glen, as seen in this 1912 photograph. (Courtesy of Frances Kreman Olbricht.)

PUBLISHED BY ARCADIA
WWW.ARCADIAPUBLISHING.COM

SECTION FOREMAN'S HOME

NEBRASKA'S COWBOY RAIL LINE

Section crews were paid to perform regular maintenance on stretches of track assigned to them. They inspected rails to ensure they were stable, replaced rotted ties, and rebuilt roadbeds where necessary. Pictured is the section foreman's home near the tracks at Glen. (Courtesy of Frances Kreman Olbricht.)

Excerpted from Images of Rail: Nebraska's Cowboy Rail Line, published by Arcadia Publishing. © 2009 Keith Terry.

PUBLISHED BY ARCADIA
WWW.ARCADIAPUBLISHING.COM

SHEFFIELD VELOCIPEDE

NEBRASKA'S COWBOY RAIL LINE

This photograph, taken at Scribner, shows what appears to be a Sheffield velocipede. These inspection cars were intended to be used by a company's road master to examine sections of track. Ideally one person would supply the power leaving another to make notes of defects in alignment along the way. (Courtesy of the Musbach Museum.)

PUBLISHED BY ARCADIA
WWW.ARCADIAPUBLISHING.COM

VALENTINE BRIDGE

NEBRASKA'S COWBOY RAIL LINE

After only 27 years of use, the bridge leading into Valentine was replaced because a pathway from one side of the river and through the Big Cut was inclined. In 1910, construction crews started on the replacement bridge a short distance from the old one. This photograph shows the completed structure. (Courtesy of Ron Hand.)

Excerpted from Images of Rail: Nebraska's Cowboy Rail Line, published by Arcadia Publishing. © 2009 Keith Terry.

PUBLISHED BY ARCADIA
WWW.ARCADIAPUBLISHING.COM

Fort Niobrara near Valentine was used from 1880 until the very early 1900s. During that time, it was home to cavalry and foot soldiers. This photograph may show the 12th Infantry preparing to leave for Cuba during the Spanish-American War. (Photograph by C.M. Eads, courtesy of Valentine's Centennial Hall.)

Excerpted from *Images of Rail: Nebraska's Cowboy Rail Line*, published by Arcadia Publishing © 2009 Keith Terry.

PUBLISHED BY ARCADIA
WWW.ARCADIAPUBLISHING.COM

HORSE TRACK

NEBRASKA'S COWBOY RAIL LINE

Neligh had a reputation as having a first-class horse-racing track, and it is visible to the right of the train in this photograph. The barn at bottom right of this 1912 photograph was owned by John Kay, a nationally prominent horse breeder, and the name of one of his champions adorns the roof. (Courtesy of the Antelope County Historical Society.)

Excerpted from Images of Rail: Nebraska's Cowboy Rail Line, published by Arcadia Publishing. © 2009 Keith Terry.

PUBLISHED BY ARCADIA
WWW.ARCADIAPUBLISHING.COM

Once the railed road extended its reach, the days of using carts, wagons, and buggies for long distance travel were numbered. Trains dramatically shortened the time required to move humans and their cargo from place to place. At the same time, they helped diffuse new innovations and ideas throughout the country. (Courtesy of Audrey Olson.)

Excerpted from Images of Rail: Nebraska's Cowboy Rail Line; published by Arcadia Publishing © 2009 Keith Terry.

PUBLISHED BY ARCADIA
WWW.ARCADIAPUBLISHING.COM

A 1913 Chicago and Northwestern newspaper ad read, "To Chicago and the East via the Northwestern line. Enjoy every minute of the trip. Superb daily trains via the direct route. Latest Pullman sleeping cars, standard day coaches and free reclining chair cars. Fast and convenient schedules." (Courtesy of Audrey Olson.)

PUBLISHED BY ARCADIA
WWW.ARCADIAPUBLISHING.COM

In the late 1800s and early 1900s, farmers and ranchers in towns in Rock and Holt Counties shipped enormous quantities of hay around the country. (Courtesy of Audrey Olson.)

Excerpted from Images of Rail: Nebraska's Cowboy Rail Line, published by Arcadia Publishing. © 2009 Keith Terry.

PUBLISHED BY ARCADIA
WWW.ARCADIAPUBLISHING.COM

TRAVELING COW AND HEN EXHIBIT   NEBRASKA'S COWBOY RAIL LINE

At one time, dairy livestock from a University of Nebraska–owned farm were loaded onto railcars and moved around the state. Once halted, faculty members gave presentations on caring for animals, identifying the qualities of a good milking cow, and diseases and their cures. This photograph, taken in Atkinson, shows a car with a "UN Cow-Hen Exhibit" sign on its side. (Courtesy of Gary A. Lech.)

Excerpted from Images of Rail: Nebraska's Cowboy Rail Line, published by Arcadia Publishing. © 2009 Keith Terry.

PUBLISHED BY ARCADIA
WWW.ARCADIAPUBLISHING.COM

SUSTENANCE AND SATISFACTION

NEBRASKA'S COWBOY RAIL LINE

The trains that traveled the route carried commodities that were desired by citizens in the region including hay, building supplies, milk, beer, ice, and livestock. Eventually they were transporting automobiles and trucks to dealers in towns along the way. As such, they assisted in their own eventual demise. (Courtesy of the Nebraska Railroad Museum.)

Excerpted from Images of Rail: Nebraska's Cowboy Rail Line, published by Arcadia Publishing © 2009 Keith Terry.

 PUBLISHED BY ARCADIA
WWW.ARCADIAPUBLISHING.COM

MAP SEARCH

Arcadia Publishing is the leading local history publisher in the United States. With more than 4,000 titles in print and hundreds of new titles released every year, Arcadia has extensive specialized experience chronicling the history of communities and celebrating America's hidden stories, bringing to life the people, places, and events from the past. To discover the history of other communities across the nation, please visit:

www.arcadiapublishing.com

Customized search tools allow you to find regional history books about the town where you grew up, the cities where your friends and family live, the town where your parents met, or even that retirement spot you've been dreaming about.

A-86866

POST CARD

MESSAGE MAY BE WRITTEN ON THIS SIDE.   ADDRESS ONLY ON THIS SIDE.

Theo. Sohmer Los Angeles

N ebraska's Cowboy Rail Line boasts a rich history. In this collection of vintage-photograph postcards, Keith Terry explores the line's past.

PUBLISHED BY ARCADIA
WWW.ARCADIAPUBLISHING.COM

$7.99

ISBN-13 978-0-7385-7709-8
ISBN-10 0-7385-7709-X

50799

9 780738 577098